Pimp to Preacher

Evangelism 911

With a Former L.A. Pimp

Bruce Henderson

Pimp to Preacher
Evangelism 911 With a Former L.A. Pimp
Copyright © 2013 by Bruce Henderson

ISBN-13: 978-1484029374
ISBN-10: 1484029372

Vienna Schilling Books
Fair Oaks, California
www.viennaschilling.us

Printed in the United States of America

Meet the Author

My name is Stanley Bruce Henderson, Jr. I'm a street preacher and evangelist for the Gospel of Jesus Christ, and a former Los Angeles pimp. I would like to share with you my testimony that means so much to me. They are events that brought me into the saving knowledge of Christ. So sit back, relax, and open your heart, as I share my life story. The Holy Spirit is our life's direction and promise of the Father.

Father, I pray that every ear and heart is open to the word of my testimony, to inspire hope, healing, destiny and most of all, God's love. It's all about the kingdom in You.

Table of Contents

PART 1

The Game

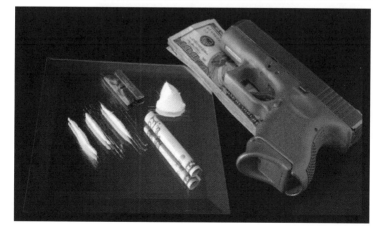

Darkness of night

With the moon shining bright

There's a set goin' strong

Lota' things goin' on

The man of the hour

Has an air of great power

The dudes have envied him for so long

Superfly

Curtiss Mayfield, Superfly

Chapter 1

The Freeway Shooting

In 1975, I was a very busy pimp. Pimpin' out my hos, runnin' guns 'n drugs, evading the cops and organizing money-making sex-parties, so on and so forth, requires a lot energy, business scruples and full-time attention.

Every five-mile radius has its own *Superfly*, and it just so happens, I was The Fly of my particular radius. Through my pimp business I earned several thousand dollars *each day*, which came in handy since I had to buy a new car every few weeks to scramble the cops. I also carried a gun 24/7, which I affectionately referred to as my 'Piece Maker' (spelling intended).

One day in 1975, four of us drove in a car along the 101 Freeway on our way to make a 'product pick up' so to speak. My long-time, drug-runner buddy was driving, I was in the passenger seat, and two lovely ladies were in the back seat, and everything seemed chill'--for the moment. Then, all of a sudden while driving the car, my buddy flipped out, literally. He had consumed way too many drugs that day and suddenly lost his mind right there on the 101 freeway. He began to shout and spew unintelligible, hysterical things at the top of his lungs. I looked at him and his eyes were tightly shut as he blindly careened the car across the freeway lanes, driving the car at high speed with his eyes shut!

"Shut your eyes, Bruce!" he shouted. "If we don't shut our eyes, we won't find the exit!"

I shouted, "What?" as he bounced us around at high speed.

"Shut up Bruce, and close your eyes! If we don't close our eyes, we won't find the exit!"

I looked up saw the exit in question zoom by at high speed with a blur, but he didn't care. Still driving blindly, he shouted, "Shut up, Bruce! Close your eyes!"

By now the two ladies sitting in the back seat screamed in terror. Needless to say, they couldn't keep their eyes shut either, preferring to die with their eyes wide open. My friend was so messed up on drugs, nothing he said made any sense! How could anyone close

their eyes when we were being bounced around by a man driving like a bat out of hell? Now, the ladies started screaming, "Let Bruce drive! Let Bruce drive!" After several minutes inside this death-trap, he pulled over onto the shoulder of the freeway, but not to let me drive. He had other plans. Walking to back of the car, he popped open the trunk and pulled out an M-14 rifle, and a sixty-round banana clip. Jamming the clip into the weapon, he started shooting at the passing cars on the freeway.

I told the ladies to get out of the car, run behind the bushes off the freeway shoulder and lie down on their stomachs. By now, he had hit several cars so I jumped him from behind as he aimed at the cars. He was very tall; six-foot, six inches, but I was stronger. The possibility that he was going to kill us all was too ominous, so I had to do something. It was a life or death situation.

I grabbed the rifle and both of our hands were on it. I was able to turn the gun toward the hills once I got leverage in front of him. I fell on top of the gun, and shot toward the mountains, beating his trigger-finger on the black top until all the bullets ran out.

Now, he was on my back, which surely meant the end of me, so the only thing that came out of my mouth was, "Jesus is coming!" That made him blink and stand up. All four doors of the car were still wide open so he jumped back in. Inexplicably, the ladies jumped back in and he drove off with women screaming once again in the back seat.

Now I ran along the shoulder of the freeway by myself. I couldn't understand why all the motorists were slowing down, looking at me in sheer terror, and then\ scramble off with their cars in every direction. Then I realized the rifle was still in my hands. It was me they were trying to escape. So, I hid the rifle in the weeds on the freeway.

I kept running until I found a phone booth. People were already calling 911 to report the freeway shooting. While in the phone booth, the LAPD police cars and helicopters surrounded me. I was talking to the police on the phone and stepped out with my hands in the air. I tried to tell them that I was the one *reporting* the shooting but they didn't care.

"Get on the ground and put your hands behind your head! Do it now! Get on the ground now!"

Chapter 2

Bruce 'Heffner'

With all guns squarely pointed at me, one of the cops finally took the phone and confirmed my 911 call. The freeway shooting came on the news that night. One man was shot in the shoulder and five cars were hit, but no one was killed. They called me a hero. They said that I saved lives, plus my own, but I was just incredibly tired. Yeah, I was a hero, alright; with a missing key of cocaine in the car that got away.

So, that was a really bad pimp-day in my private pimp-world, but I had good pimp-days as well. One late-summer morning, I was in my plush, player apartment, fast asleep when a knock came at my door. I stood up naked, grabbed a pillow and held it in front of my per-sonals to go and open the door. There stood two beauti-ful, young ladies at seven o'clock in the morning yelling,

"Happy Birthday!" My spirits were immediately brightened. They were gay-girlfriends that worked for me, whose private girl-on-girl show was in high demand by all my clients, and on this particular morning, they had a number of surprises in store for me.

"Just relax baby! We're gonna' take care of everything! We're gonna' make you breakfast and give you a shower!"

"Or a bath if you like," said the other doll.

So they got undressed and led me into the shower and we all jumped in. We had such a great time that morning washing each other, laughing and being silly. They were cute, street-smart and intelligent, and really knew how to treat a pimp.

It was now a few hours later and a regular stream of women entered my place. The girls that worked for me were awesome people with lots of personality, lots of bravado. Mine was a luxury apartment with a swimming pool and bar, fully stocked with every drink mix you could think of and that day, there was no shortage of money coming my way. Each lady that came to the party brought me gifts, money, pleasure and liquor.

Before long, I looked up and counted thirty-five gorgeous, sexy women milling about my place, pampering and seducing me. It was good to be the Big Daddy Mac, and I enjoyed every minute of it. Girls were in the pool in bikinis and sexy swimwear of all types, thumping music played loudly on the stereo, alcohol and drugs flowed freely. Then they sang *Happy Birthday* to me. Some girls were new to my stable, others were veterans, and yet they all managed to get together and plan the party weeks ahead of time. I was Bruce 'Heffner' for the day.

Back then, my business model, if you will, was simple but effective: throw a lot of parties in the large apartment that I and my partners owned, invite a lot of celebrities and VIPs, and keep our girls working. Well into the night, everyone got naked, drank alcohol, consumed drugs, engaged in illicit sex and forked over the cash. The only things missing were Roman togas.

On one particular occasion, one of my special girls caught a rich man's eye. He was from Japan and she was very smart by always gravitating toward the rich. We worked well together and shared the same appreciation for the dollar. She also hosted a well-known, celebrity client list that I can't talk about.

Now, the rich man invited her to Japan, and whenever she returned to the United States, he sent her large sums of money every week, in the form of Yen, the Japanese currency, which we converted into the U.S. dollar. Needless to say, I made lots of money from the beautiful nation of Japan.

Then, my special girl got into trouble during one of her trips to Japan. She was busted at the airport with a marijuana joint that someone gave her in Japan, and they don't play around in Japan when it comes to that sort of thing. They bring your accuser right up to your face and she went to jail for a month. The Japanese jail system requires that you stay in a small circle while doing your time, and you cannot step out of the circle. If you do, they punish you.

Back in the 1970s, a very good friend of mine made a lot of Black movies, some of which you probably know...*Sparkle, Bingo Long, Car Wash*, and many more. I remember my actor friends and I going to a disco in the Marina called the *Dragon Fly*. Lots of women were there, but nobody was dancing. Most people don't want to be the first one on the floor. The *Dragon Fly* was a spacious club and the D.J. played a lot of nice music, but nobody got up to dance. Then, the D.J. played *Bad Luck* by Teddy Pendergrass, and that's when I got on the dance floor. Being the natural party-man that I am, I stretched out my hands to the thirty-plus woman still sitting at their lonely tables and called out to them, "Let's dance! C'mon, let's dance!" but nobody moved. So, remembering my sense of humor, I told them:

"Okay, so I'll dance for you!"

And then I tore it up. I did the splits, the break-down, the robot and moon-walk, right there in front of them. I gave them *a show!*

My friends could not believe it. After that, all the women asked me to dance one after the other, and as I turned to leave, the ladies didn't want me to go and yelled out, "No, you *can't go* now!"

There was a line of women waiting to dance with me. What can I say? When you got it, you got it. You just have to know how to play the game.

Chapter 3

A Day at the Office

I had a lot of respect for the mob. I liked their business model. 1) Walk into a business...2) Demand a percentage of the owner's income...3) Threaten violence if he doesn't comply...4) Collect the cash once a month.

The mob makes local business owners offers that they couldn't refuse, which I also admired. If the owners didn't comply they found their store windows and inventory smashed to bits; but they also did a lot of 'good' for them, if that's what you'd like to call it. For instance, if the business owner needs little extra operating cash, he could ask the mob to stage a robbery and destroy a portion of his store, for which he filed a claim with his insurance company, whereupon the insurance adjuster came out, assessed the damage and a few days later, handed the owner a hefty check for thousands of dollars to pay for 'the damages' -- of which the mob collects a percentage for the 'artistic production' they staged. However, such services are available only to their best-paying customers.

Store owners loved me. In exchange for partnership I offered them cash, clothing, jewelry, connections with diamond importers and wealthy dealers of big-ticket, quality merchandise of all kinds, such as stolen, new cars. Most of the stores that I 'partnered' with were in Beverly Hills and Hollywood, so we're talking about hundreds of thousands of dollars,

People love money. A smart (but demented) business owner knows that if you run a game in your own store, you double your money. We also had an endless stream of new credit cards, received straight from our operatives inside the post office. But wait; there's more!

We also had bus drivers on our payroll. In partnership with us, they hit cars and created crashes. The bus drivers received immunity (because accidents came with the job), while the injured party filed personal injury law suits, which became 'fast money' through our attorneys. I got paid up front to 'produce' the accident, while everyone inside the car got paid later down the line; about

$3,500 each. We did one a day and it was just another day at the office for us.

Two friends that I knew from high school came to me one day and said, "We got to move." They were talking about doing a job. They needed a car and meant to get one. So we found a good tunnel beneath a freeway and waited. They got out of the car to look for prospects while I stayed in the cut as the get-away driver. Back then I owned a fast, luxury car and always kept my gun close by. After a few minutes they came running out of the tunnel. One of them had a limp, but the boy flew out like a race horse. I sped up and opened the door. They jumped in and lay down on the floor with a big bag of money. That's all folks!

Still running the game, my cousin and I went out one evening in Westwood. There was a live band at a club for a basically all-white crowd, except for one other Black couple; significant because the stage was now set for easy prey. We all got on the floor and started dancing when one of the white ladies asked me, "What's your friend's name over there?"

I said, "Wilson," whereupon she gushed, "Oh, so that *is him*!"

Then she told everyone in the club and people sent drinks over to us. They asked the band if 'Wilson Pickett' could sing with them, but the band leader said, "We can't just let anyone come up here and sing," but the crowd persisted, "But he's Wilson Pickett!"

That's when they invited 'Wilson Pickett' onto the stage. Now, my friend whispered to me, "But I don't know any of his songs that well!"

To compensate for 'Wilson Pickett' not knowing his own songs, I told the crowd that I was his manager.

"He's under contract and can't do original songs!"

When you play the game, you have to be quick on your feet. So he sang many Marvin Gaye songs and a few other artists. Everyone in the club was on the dance floor. They didn't want him to stop singing until the club closed. At closing time, one of the ladies at the club approached me and said, "I just got my income tax refund of $2,500. Is that enough to go with you?"

What do you think? Gangsters, drug-dealers, pimps, robbers, imposters; just another day at the office.

Chapter 4

Competition:

My Favorite Snack

One of my best customers who bought drugs from me, got arrested, went to jail for a couple of weeks, and later made bail. Upon her release, she called me for help to get back on her feet. Nobody would help her but me. I gave her drugs to sell on consignment and told her to pay me back at the end of the month. About three or four days later, she came back with stacks of money that she owed me.

"Baby, I don't want you doing anything. I will take care of you," she said. Her team hooked up with my team and it was on. We made a lot of money by delivering drugs every evening in shopping bags, like groceries. We worked well together without distractions because

Bruce Henderson

she was gay, which kept her mind on business. One night, we were out making deliveries when the police pulled her over for running a red light while looking for an address. I was in the car with her, and gave her the instructions.

"Don't panic; just unbutton your shirt all the way down."

"For what?"

"To distract the cop."

And it worked. She never wore a bra and had very large breasts. The cop actually forgot what he pulled us over for because he was looking directly at her breasts the whole time. He let us go without further complication or delay.

She told him, "I should give you a big kiss!"

And he actually put his head through the window and let her kiss him on the cheek.

Months later, she asked me to go with her to an all-gay party for women. I wondered if they would even let me in so she said, "If they don't want you, they don't want me!" But, of course, I was welcomed. They had heard about me. There were approximately fifty women there, dancing and having fun until the sound system failed and they had no music. They tried to fix it, but couldn't. I offered to take a look at it, and victory again; I fixed it, of course. Most of the women asked me to dance and some were slipping their phone number in my hand while dancing. I guess they weren't *that gay*, after all.

Two of my boys from the 'hood got involved with two, biological sisters from Washington, D.C.; beautiful, curvaceous white girls, eighteen and twenty years of age, with long, silky, brunet hair.

My boys were silly dope fiends and didn't know what to do with these girls. They were handsome, but had no brains. I came through for these girls a couple of times and they chose me to be their 'manager' and dumped my boys. Yeah sure, they were angry but there was nothing they could do about it.

The two white girls were super freaks...the kind you don't take home to mother. I walked in on them one day doing each other and I told them, "Guys would pay you *a lot of money* to watch you freak off with each other." So I scheduled a long, distinguished line of clientele, after which they liked putting on the show so much, it became their favorite pastime. They made me lots of money throughout Hollywood and Beverly Hills.

Competition: My Favorite Snack

These white-girl sisters were characters, funny joke-sters, which was good for the line of business we were in. Humor makes everything more enjoyable as long as you could manage to keep it. They were not hard to please and I knew how to keep them happy. So that was me back in the day. I had a gift of catching women and attracting money, lots of it.

A friend of mine tried to catch a certain woman for months without success; apparently, she just wouldn't give it up. So he pointed her out to me at a club one night and made me a bet that I couldn't get her. Long story short, I left with the woman about an hour later. She invited me to her home, a nice, spacious home, and the rest is history.

That's how the game goes. I knew how to play cops, co-workers, friends, enemies and everyone in between. Everyone was competition – my favorite snack.

A few years later, I was at a club and a certain woman kept looking over at me from across the room. She waived at me to get my attention and from across the room she mouthed the words...*Did I sleep with you?* She was with a date, some poor, unsuspecting slob, as she tried hide her words behind a wine glass. I didn't recognize her for a minute but then it dawned on me. It was the same woman my friend lost the bet over. She was still fine, but had cut her hair. It was funny watching her gestures from across the room; like watching comedy.

Competition, however, did come with a price. Friends are always around when the weather is fair, but what about when dark clouds roll in? Do they stick around?

I was having a small party one evening at my apartment with eight people. There were plenty of drugs, liquor and paraphernalia all over the apartment and our party had become perhaps a little too loud. Suddenly, someone buzzed my apartment's intercom system. I answered and it was the police.

Through the intercom, I asked them, "Do you have a search warrant?" They had no answer to that question but I knew it didn't do any good. They didn't need one to make a simple house call. So, I went downstairs and saw two cops standing at the door; one white and the other Black. The Black cop asked, "Are you the one who asked about the search warrant?"

"Yes."

So he lifted his foot in the air and said, "This size thirteen shoe is my warrant." So, I said, "Come on up," hoping my guests hid all the drugs by now. When the cops walked into my apartment, the drugs were all over the floor and table. Everyone was gone.

The Black cop said, "Well, it looks like your friends didn't clean up so good, and now you're going to jail." He took a closer look at the drugs on the table and added, "Dangerous drugs too! Better get your toothbrush." In cop-speak, this means, "You're going away for a long time."

Boldly I announced, "I don't need it," referring to the toothbrush. Once downstairs at the police car, the Black cop said, "Stretch out your hands on the car."

My mother told me about the Lord many times so, hysterically, I started praying out loud as I sat in the police car. It was both tragic and comical. Then, the Black cop said, "Let's go back upstairs." I didn't know what for, but as soon as we walked into my apartment, the cop handed my drugs back to me.

He walked me into the bathroom and said, "Now, flush it down the toilet." I did so and he left. God showed me His rescue that night but I was still a fool for a long time after that.

PART 2

The Visitations

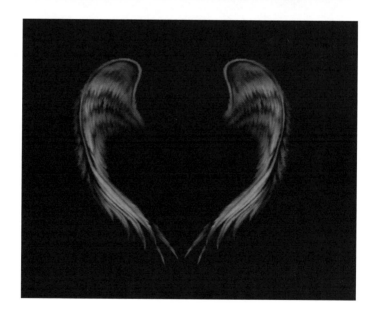

So the last will be first, and the first last. For many are called, but few are chosen."

Matthew 20:16

Chapter 5

Losing My Marbles

One day at the very height of my pimpdom, I made the mistake of stopping over at my mother's house located on 48th Street, in Los Angeles, when she handed me a little booklet, entitled *Devil You Can't Hurt Me, I'm God's Property!* written by the late, great Oral Roberts.

I wish she hadn't done that. My mother stood there in the kitchen with a hand on her hip and said, "Bruce, read this because *I know* what you' doin'!"

I never admitted to any of my atrocities, but like so many other long-suffering ghetto-mothers, I knew that she knew. And she knew that I knew that she knew, too, but I never admitted to what she already knew.

That particular day I drove home with the little booklet in my back pocket, which soon proved to pack a big punch.

I drove to one of the places where I hid my stash, went inside and irreverently threw the booklet on the table. I wrapped up my stash and got ready to leave. As I headed for the door, I turned and looked at the booklet. Suddenly a light went on in my heart and mind. I picked it up, sat on the couch and actually read it. The small booklet shared the word of God, His love and His power. At first I read one page, then another and another. I forgot about the stash in my coat and my customers waiting for it. In fact, I forgot all time and space.

That unsuspecting afternoon, I burst out crying and could not stop. I was convicted of all the things that I ever did, and yet I felt no hard finger pointed in my face. It was a tender conviction that melted away my layers of sin and arrogance and bravado, until I was nothing more than a little, naked baby held by the nail-scarred hands of the Lord. When I finished the booklet, I said, "Lord help me, and change me."

I had fifteen to twenty girls working for me back then, depending on who was on duty; working Hollywood, Long Beach and Beverly Hills. It was my living and source of income. At the time I earned between $50,000 to $80,000 a month and I had no idea, nor the fortitude how to change that or give it up. The Lord Himself would have to splice the universe in two and set me on a new course; and that's exactly what He did.

Shortly after reading that booklet, I went to visit a friend who had a large tray of what appeared to be cocaine on his coffee table, but it wasn't; it was a new, potent drug, a new deadly mix, and I sniffed a dose into each nostril, whereupon the drainage of the drug began to burn against my throat tissue. In fact, it burned so badly that I ran to the bathroom and tried to vomit, but it wouldn't expel. Then, the airway in my throat began to close up and my head got tighter. Without oxygen going to my brain, I blacked out. All I could do was think, *I'm going to die.*

By now my friend was panicked and pounded on the bathroom door. "Hey man, are you okay? Need any help?"

I fell back against the wall, slid down to the floor, chocking. All that came to my mind was the little booklet my mother had given me. *Devil You Can't Hurt Me, I'm God's Property!* So, I kept repeating that over and over in my mind, even with my last breath. *Devil, you can't hurt me. I'm God's property!*

And then I hit the ground. I stopped breathing for about three to five minutes. Then, inexplicably, I came back to life, but something strange was happening. I was speaking in tongues. My tongue moved very quickly and fiercely with an unknown language bursting through my mouth in rapid, quick-fire succession over which I had no control.

I had only heard of tongues but never really knew what it was. The word of God states in the Book of Mark 16:17-18, "And these signs will follow those who believe: in My name they will drive out demons and speak in new tongues. They will pick up deadly things with their hands, and when they drink deadly poison, it will not hurt them at all. They will place their hands on the sick, and they will recover."

The Lord filled me with His Holy Spirit that day. When I came back to life on the bathroom floor, I continued to speak in tongues for several minutes. After the tongues stopped, I heard a strange noise, audibly, in my belly. It was something like a whirlwind deep down inside my being. I felt millions of particles forming together in my belly, and the whirling action made a terrific, loud noise; as though rocks were being racked up together in my belly. And then, something shot up into my mouth. From my mouth plunged a beautiful marble of vibrant colors; black, white, yellow. The marble was a perfect, flawless sphere. After the beautiful marble fell out of my mouth, I held it in my hand and looked at it for several minutes, bewildered. Then I threw it in the toilet.

As soon as the marble plopped into the toilet water, the Lord arrested my spirit and my eyes were opened. I watched as the bathroom walls disintegrated, exposing a hundred, grotesque spirits of darkness loitering about my friend's apartment. These were shape-shifters and man-eaters, the soul-destroyers of all mankind and it seemed they were called to order in that house. Even in my drug fog and lustful self-absorption, I knew that I was being a granted a visitation from the Holy One.

Demons are real. I could hear them talking, communicating with each other. Some sat on the tables, others crouched in corners and on top of furniture. Clearly, this was their domain. The vision lasted for at least a minute, which was a long time to be trapped in that setting.

Still in the bathroom, the Lord let me see another vision. About forty to fifty of the same demons were walking around a huge, black pot, as big as an apartment building. The demons pranced back-to-back, as though in a ritual. As I looked up, I saw fire shooting out from the top of the black pot. The Bible speaks of the pit of hell; that deep, fire and brimstone cavern where lost souls languish in agony for all eternity. This was just a small portion of hell.

Finally out of the vision but still in the bathroom, I'm ready to leave, still alive and breathing. As I opened the door, there was my buddy.

I said, "What were you trying to do, kill me?"

He assured me that he was not. In fact, he called his mother, who lived only a few doors down, to quickly come and pray for me. The young man looked at me and said, while I was in the bathroom, he heard me preaching. He said that I sounded like a seasoned preacher with power. So there I stood with all of them looking at me, and that's when it became crystal clear.

"I'm okay," I said. "I don't know any scriptures, but I do know that I'm a new creature."

I just had a collision with the Holy Ghost and survived. From that moment forward, everything was different. Suddenly, the world was full of purpose.

Suddenly, I knew that I was here for a reason. You can't figure it out with the natural mind, it was just a feeling I had, a new awareness of myself and all creation. It takes over the whole person. I felt whole for the first time in my life. I had become a new creation, but the process was not overnight.

Chapter 6

Invisible Intruder

After that, I drove home to my apartment located at 43rd and Wilton Avenue, deep in the heart of Los Angeles. With this power still upon me, I got out of my car and noticed two men standing against the side of my apartment building. I walked upstairs to my apartment whereupon I saw two more men at the end of the hallway. Unbeknownst to me, there was a hit on my life.

I put the key into the lock, entered my apartment and took a shower. At the time, my hair was extremely long down to my shoulders. When I stepped out of the shower, I began to trim my beard and looked in the mirror. Then I heard an audible voice say, "Go!"

Just as it states in the Bible, it was a voice of a multitude, a voice of many waters. Then I heard it again. "Go!" It was right inside my head, and the feeling I got was one of precise, divine direction, an instant knowledge of whose voice it was. Creation knows its creator. However, instead of obeying the voice, I continued trimming my beard.

This time, the power fell upon me again and, threw the razor out of my hand. Time and space again evaporated at that moment as I watched the razor fall into the sink in slow-motion, frame by frame motion, like taking snapshots of many pictures. Then I saw the water splash in slow motion.

The power then began pushing me toward the door. I had just gotten out of the shower and didn't have clothes on, so I walked into my closet, to reach for my clothes but a second audible voice said, "You don't have time!"

Later I realized that the men loitering about my apartment had probably come to kill me. It was a danger not uncommon in my industry, with rival pimps walking up to the other pimp's car, and shooting them right there at the intersection, in broad daylight.

And so the power pushed me toward the door, comically, just like in the movies when you can't see the ghost pushing the character. When I got to the front door I reached for the door knob and it stopped me again. I was naked and the voice said, "No! You will be ashamed!" That was the third audible voice of God.

The invisible power spun me around and walked me toward my bed, whereupon it pulled the sheet off my bed, literally, opened it up like a large, billowing sail, and wrapped it around me without my lifting a finger. Shrouded in the bed-sheet, the power again pushed me toward the front door which opened on its own. I didn't have shoes on; I was barefoot.

Once my foot stepped outside the door, I saw that some kind of pillar of fire walked with me. I looked down at my feet and hands and they were ablaze with light, as though fire were upon them. I looked at my side, to the right and left, and now I saw walls of fire. When I looked up, I saw more fire roaring above me. The Bible states the Lord is a consuming fire. I didn't know about this scripture at the time, but I experienced it in living color. And so I fire-walked down the stairs and proceeded toward my mother's house, about a half-hour journey on foot.

Walking down the street in bare feet, with long, wet hair, wearing nothing but a sheet, the average on-looker must have thought I had lost my mind.

"Look at him! He must think he's Jesus Christ!" some might have said. It was now about 4:30 P.M. in the late afternoon. My mother had given me the booklet, *Devil You Can't Hurt me, I'm God's Property!* only the day before and already I could barely recognize my life.

I never saw those men again. God was my invisible intruder and there was no further room for them.

Chapter 7

Mama, Don't Shoot Me!

Divinely led back to my mother's house, engulfed by this holy fire and shrouded in my bed sheet, I could not stop walking. I walked briskly and succinctly acutely aware of everyone and everything around me.

Once at my mother's house, I knocked on the door, and you can imagine what happened next. At the sight of me, she wailed loudly, "Oh Lord, my son has gone crazy!"

She ran to wake up my father who was napping in the back room. He came out, took a close look at me and said, "No, I can tell Bruce is not high. He's talking very clearly."

My mother insisted all this looked very strange, and threatened to get out her gun. I had been saved less than two hours and didn't know how to articulate what happened to me, so I didn't. Furthermore, had I told my parents all about it, would they think my story was crazier than the bed-sheet? So I did the only thing I knew to do. As a practiced liar all my life, I lied to her again.

"Mom, I made a bet with someone and won; that's all. So go and get your gun if it makes you feel comfortable. Get your gun, because I agree, it does look strange."

So she went and got her gun, laid it on the kitchen table and sat across from me, looking at me intently. I sat there still naked beneath my bed-sheet and we started talking.

Shaking her head in disbelief, she asked, "What have you got on, under that bed-sheet?"

"Nothin'."

"Oh my God!" she gasped.

"Let me go into my old room and get some clothes on?"

On the way down the hall, I went into the bathroom to wash my feet. Remember, I was barefoot and had walked a mile through dirt, gravel, soot and oily street grime. I sat on the tub, lifted my feet to wash them, and saw that there was not one spec of dirt on them! Instead, my feet were shining and glowing. In fact, they bore the high sheen and glow of a brand new, silver dollar. *Wow!* What can say or think at times like that? I didn't show my parents my feet because I was not sure what to make of it myself at that point, plus it would only lead to questions that I didn't know how to answer just yet.

I spent the night at my mother's house and, laying there on my childhood bed, the Lord lifted me into yet another vision. This time I saw the world burning up and being destroyed. Planet Earth was engulfed in screaming, hellish flames. Unlike the gentle, impenetrable fire that surrounded me earlier that day, this angry fire destroyed everything in its path.

The next morning I was ready to walk back home when my father came up to me and said, "Son, let me give you a ride." I politely declined but he insisted. I left that day without telling my parents what had really happened. I would not tell them about it for another year, but my mother knew I was hiding something and continued to ask me about the incident over the next year. In fact, she couldn't let it go.

My mother was full of spit and polish. She made no effort to be hilarious and yet her spritely audacity made her the funniest person I ever knew. Street-smart and bold, she filled my childhood with old, colloquial sayings that I barely understood, only that she meant business when she said them.

"Love many, trust few; always paddle your own canoe!"

"Papa didn't kill the hog for the hair; he kill' it for the meat."

"Nobody want a bone but a dog; and he go' bury it!"

"Nothin' ruins a duck but it's own beck!"

On this day she had no sayings of antiquity. She just let her gun do the talking. After my father dropped me off at my apartment, I saw one of my neighbors and she hollered out, "Bruce, are you okay?"

She came up to me and breathless, she said, "Last night I had a dream about you! I dreamed that you died in the street with a sheet on!" I stood there bewildered, listening as she described what she saw in the dream.

"I went upstairs to your apartment and knocked on the door. The door was half-way opened and I got really scared. Then, I saw a light on inside and I kept calling your name...*Bruce, Bruce!*...but there was no answer. So, I went in and turned off the light. On my way out, I hollered, '*Okay, I'll see you later!* So in my dream I closed your door and went back downstairs."

What an awesome God He is. I took this to mean that the pillar of fire blazing all around me yesterday on the street no doubt protected me from the imminent killing spree against my life. And yet, one would think that after all that, I would get my life together, but there's just something about the flesh that resists the notion. The Bible states, "There is no good thing in the flesh."

Shortly after my day of visions and not yet knowing how to get out of the drug trade, I went to deliver an order of drugs in the Crenshaw district of Los Angeles. (The customer was the daughter of a well-known, state official.) After the delivery, I drove away down Stocker Street, ready to make a right turn, when the power of God showed up in my car. The power spun the steering wheel to the left. As I write of these nuclear events, the hair on my head stands up.

This time I did not hear an audible voice, so I said out loud, "Lord, where are you taking me?" I was unaware that the Holy Ghost knows how to drive a car!

By the time I got to 39th and Crenshaw, I just sat behind the wheel with my hands in my lap, watching the steering wheel turn to the left and right, as the Holy Ghost drove my car. The car then turned and stopped in front of a familiar radio station. I asked the Lord if he wanted me to get out, but I didn't hear anything. I have an engineering license in radio broadcasting and quite often visited my good friend who worked there.

Eventually, I got out of the car and went inside. When my friend saw me, he hollered, "Bruce, you made it to the party!" I was not even aware that there was a party. The power of God led me there.

I started talking to a few people, mixing and mingling. Then I looked up toward the door and a man walked in that stood as tall as the door, about six feet-eight or nine inches, and he had a smile on his face. He was a Black man wearing black jeans and a plaid shirt. He kept staring at me, so I waved at him and he waved back; but he just kept starring. This freaked me out a little, and I wondered, *What's going on?* He came over and introduced himself as 'Michael.'

He said, "Let me tell you what this is all about. It's about the sixty-six books." Then, he said, "I have to go now, but I will see you again."

At the time, I had no clue what he meant by 'the sixty-six books,' but today I do. He was referring to the thirty-nine books of the Old Testament, and the twenty-seven books in the New Testament. Do the math, and it comes to sixty-six. Then he turned around and walked out the door. I followed after him but once outside I didn't see him, or anything to even suggest that he was ever there. I found myself running around the entire building of the radio station, and up the street to Crenshaw Boulevard looking for this tall guy, who stood head and shoulders above everyone else. If I was only seconds behind him, how could I miss him? Because I shot after him so quickly, at the very least I should have seen him just as he got into his car, or pulled out the driveway, but he had disappeared into thin air.

Finally, I gave up and went back into the station. I found the first guy I was talking to and asked, "So, who was that tall guy?" Should I be surprised that he answered, "What tall guy?"

After asking five or six more people, nobody saw him, so I just gave up. Besides, had I persisted any longer, the other party-goers might have thought I was looking for my lover, or something. The Bible states in Hebrews 13:2, "Be not forgetful to entertain strangers, for some have unknowingly entertained angels."

The Lord did not let me go. Each and every day presented a new and different adventure, and yet, I was still involved in the sinful lifestyle. I believe this power was there to protect me, but it was also there to teach me right from wrong, in the sight of God. These events are all part of one's calling in life. Because of them, I knew that I was being 'called.' The Bible states, "Many are called, but few are chosen." As one who was just strutting along one day, minding my own business, I had definitely been chosen.

Billions of people are invited but don't want to accept Him, believing they will have to sacrifice things and get cleaned up first; when in fact, they are invited to come to Him just as they are. God is not a taker; He's a giver. The Lord understands that our vices and addictions are merely the motions of our sick flesh, and He does not condemn us for any of it. He washes them all away, if only we would come to Him, just as we are.

One day during this time, I was driving along in my car with a young lady-friend in the passenger seat. Along the way, she recognized a house where her friend lived and asked if we could stop there for just a minute, and I said, "Sure, just don't be too long. I'll wait out here."

As soon she got out of the car I started to lose my breath. Within seconds I was making gasping sounds, as though my breath left my body. Then I stopped breathing all together and my head slumped forward onto my chest. I was paralyzed and could not move, and yet my eyes stayed opened. Then a black cloud formed above my head and moved slowly down my body, engulfing my whole body in the blackness, limb by limb. Within seconds, the darkness engulfed my knees, then my arms, legs, and soon the tips of my shoes. I was now in total darkness, paralyzed and suffocating. This was not of the Lord. I was being attacked by the evil one. The devil perceives a strong calling on someone's life, and in a jealous rage, comes along to snuff it out. The Lord does not come to paralyze and suffocate; He comes to rescue.

Suddenly, I realized that I was no longer in my body. I was now hovering around in space, up around the moon and stars. In a matter of seconds, the Lord showed up to rescue me; yes, He is there, even out there in deep space. That's when He opened my airway and helped me to breathe. Now I seemed to drift more easily, and began speaking the word of the Lord. I shared my testimony to the cosmos as though to preach a sermon the entire world below could hear, and when I stopped, I knew it was perfect. The devil had come to kill me, but the Lord crushed his deep space mission, and turned it into a preaching convention, confirming to me that I was to go into all the world and preach the Gospel. You might say, it was my 'Day of Inauguration.'

Still floating in space, disembodied, I wondered, *What's going to happen next?* Through this darkness I saw a light, as though inside a tunnel, and my spirit man was being drawn ever closer toward it. The light ahead was life back on Earth. I drifted quickly toward our Blue Planet, closer and closer and from this bird's-eye view, I soon saw cars parked along the boulevards and one of the cars was mine. It was as though the Lord lowered the sky and put me right through the car and back into my body still slumped over in the seat. Next, the black cloud that first consumed me, lifted and once again I saw my feet, my legs and arms, and now daylight.

Blinking my eyes and sucking a deep tank of fresh air into my lungs, I was afraid to look around. I thought, *What happened? Did the world end?* Then the young lady came bouncing back to the car and said, "Oh you're up! I came out to invite you in but you had fallen asleep."

Little did she know I was a dead man. Counting the incident in the bathroom, the hit on my life and now this death inside my car, I had thrice cheated the Grimm Reaper, and the Lord, it seemed, would not allow me to die. I had work to do.

This is what I can say for a fact: God tells us in John 3:16, "Whosoever believes in Him shall not perish, but will have everlasting life."

Chapter 8

Fast Forward

I'm an artist. I paint and draw, and work as a professional make-up artist. During my pimpdom, I took a lot of nude photos of women and created oil paintings which I hung on my walls. One evening I was getting ready to go out and headed for the door to leave. As I approached the door, a powerful force, like a wind, blew me backward onto the ground. It scared me to death. I was laid out on the floor and watched as the nude pictures on my wall fell to the ground, one by one, from one corner of the wall to the next. All the nude pictures fell, except the ones that were not nude.

The force would not allow me to leave my apartment whereupon fear flooded over me. The first thing I said was, "Where is that Bible I stole from the hotel?"

I found the Bible and read it for most of the night, and when I got sleepy, I used the Bible as my pillow. Thinking back on these things now is like reliving every minute of them. God is a good God and the Father is not finished with me yet. He is still working on me, even today.

A day or two later, I was again in my apartment, which I used as a stash-place to hide all kind of things. On this day, the power of God fell upon me again.

I know most people have DVD/VCRs and other video equipment. If you put your DVD on fast-forward, you know how that would make the film look; right? Well, the Lord put me in fast-forward motion that day. In fact, His power caused me to move so quickly, I could barely see my hands moving. He had once again translated me into realm where there was no time or space and the normal motions of one's body were completely irrelevant.

In a matter of moments, I cleaned my whole apartment, disposed of cocaine spoons, heroine spoons, pipes and rolling papers, plastic baggies and weigh-scales. I cleaned up my whole apartment in fast-forward motion, as my hands moved so quickly, they were nothing more than a blur. The Bible speaks about the Prophet Elijah, how he outran the chariots. The power of God fell upon me in the same way, and sped me up to a hundred miles an hour to clean my entire apartment. When I stopped, I basically collapsed because that power was so intense, it drained me.

About two hours later, a friend of mine stopped by who had come to visit me many times. He was well familiar with all my nude pictures and drug paraphernalia around my apartment. So, he stood there for a long time looking around and blinking, as though to take it all in. Then he said, "Your place reminds me of a church."

No one knew what was happening to me, not even my parents, and yet these were the words that came out of his mouth. It seemed the Lord had a thing about rearranging my whole house. He had moved in and was making Himself at home. From there things changed quickly and I swam ever deeper into the river of the Lord

When the Lord has a call upon your life, there is no doubt. I always tell people, "We have a lot of counterfeit preachers today who don't have the heart of God. They don't love the people, and are all about the money." But I do know there are true callings on many men and women of God that are led by the Spirit of the Father.

Shortly thereafter, I was driving along Figueroa. It was a bright, sunny day and I was out running errands. Suddenly, I looked up in the sky and saw a beam of light flying straight toward my car. It flowed in the air and came through my window on the driver's side. The bright light flew right by me and landed on the passenger's seat next to me. I was transfixed and just praised the Lord over and over. The light was the size of a soccer ball, which then exploded into a thousand, bright sparkles that lit up the entire interior of my car. I was so excited to see this supernatural thing!

When I beheld this glowing, wondrous thing, all I could think was, *This is God's glory and presence!* I felt His love and presence very strongly during those moments, and suddenly I no longer wanted to be here on Earth. I wanted to go home and be with Him, and I kept saying over and over, "Lord take me with you, it's ugly down here! Take me with you."

Then, the light of the Lord left and vanished without a trace as though it never happened. I felt abandoned and left behind, and I cried like a baby. His presence that day was a small sampling of what we will feel for all eternity, and when His presence departs, it's such an empty feeling that you just can't describe. I never felt love like that before and there is nothing like it, here on Earth. Only God gives that kind of love and I will never forget it. His love defies all understanding and explanation.

PART 3
The Assignment

"God says, 'You are going to be great in My name! Hundreds of thousands will come to Christ because of the work that the Lord will do through you!"

Kenneth Hagin Ministries,
Los Angeles Convention Center
1986

Chapter 9

The God Clock

When I first got saved a friend of mine invited me to church, and after just a few weeks, the Lord revealed to me some shocking things about the four pastors at this particular church, standing at the pulpit, but one of them bothered me in particular.

It started with people telling me things like, "That's the pastor's girlfriend over there," which soon evolved into, "That young lady got pregnant by the pastor."

Way too many questionable things were going on at that church, and having just recently come out of the street-life, I knew this was not acceptable behavior of a pastor. So I decided to leave that whore-mongering place. Shortly thereafter, and still very early in my new, Christian walk, I stopped by a strip club, but not to drink or pick up women; it was just a routine habit that I had not yet broken. So I walked in and stood at the back looking around for a moment, just trying to unwind. Then, I looked up and saw this man jump up on the stage with a glass of liquor in his hand, dancing provocatively with the stripers. It was the assistant pastor at the church I had just left.

My instincts were correct. What made the incident particularly hard to take is that as I studied the word for myself, I later understood what great danger of hellfire these imposters are in, and how utterly destructive they are to the Body of Christ. The Bible declares many will come in the Lord's name, but inside they are like ravenous wolves dressed in sheep's clothing. We will know them by their fruit.

Two years passed and little by little the old man fell off me like a useless shell but not yet completely. The God Clock, however, had begun to tick. During this time my father kept asking me for a grandchild before he passed away so I asked my girlfriend if we could get pregnant. Before long, we brought a beautiful, baby girl into the world named Natalie Lynn, who was born in

1980. Then, our second child came along; Sha'ree Faith Henderson was born in 1986,

Natalie was born with a birth defect. Her throat wasn't fully developed and she had a short tongue. Natalie had to remain in the hospital for three months after birth. As a result of these complications, the doctors gave her a tracheotomy, which is a tube that went into her throat below the voice box, opening the airway to help her breathe. Her little tongue was so small, we could not feed her by mouth, and she had to have several surgeries.

The tracheotomy was inserted when she was just a week old, and in intensive care. One night, I was at home asleep and, at midnight, I jumped straight up out of my sleep, and drove straight to the hospital. This was an urgency from God. I had to get there without hesitation. When I arrived at intensive care, I walked over to her crib and saw that my baby had turned almost blue. She was not getting enough oxygen. She was in an incubator and I screamed out to the nurse to come quickly. It looked to me as though she was filing her nails or something, and had neglected to make her rounds like she was supposed to.

Still sitting, nurse looked up lazily and answered, "The baby was dusty," meaning, the mucous had to be suctioned out of the tracheal tube. I screamed out again, "She is dying!" The nurse finally got up out of her seat, came over and pushed the emergency button. Then, all the emergency doctors came rushing in, grabbed the incubator and rushed out. Within half an hour, one of the doctors came back and tried to explain what was happening to my baby, using excessive, medical words I couldn't understand.

I said, "Hey Doc, I could see that my baby was dying."

The doctor said, "You're right. One minute later and your baby would have died."

God has perfect timing. He's the creator and maker of all life. The God Clock never fails, nor does it ever need to be rewound.

In 1986 I was invited by a Christian lady to attend a 'camp meeting' at the Los Angeles Convention Center. I had met her at the Children's Hospital where Natalie was being treated. My friend said that I should bring Natalie to the meeting for prayer. The camp meeting was conducted by Kenneth Hagin Ministries of the Rhema Bible Training Center, located in Broken Arrow, Oklahoma. About five thousand people were in attendance and as soon as you walked in, one could feel the power of the Lord, like electric feathers floating in the air. Kenneth Hagin Ministries is well-known for its deep involvement in miracles, healing and the prophetic word. People languish for years not knowing who they are in Christ and waste their time going to churches that produce no spiritual wine and oil. No wonder they never grow in their gifts. If you want confirmation of your calling, seek out a Spirit-filled ministry where the gifts of the Holy Spirit are in *full operation*. The leaders and elders at such churches, being filled with the all-telling Holy Spirit, will immediately hear from the Lord, identify your calling and generously confirm you in front of everyone.

During the service, the time came for people to go up to the front for prayer. Just then, the prophet walked up to the microphone and said, "There is a man here tonight with a baby that has a tracheotomy! Come on up! The Lord wants to heal your baby, right now!"

I knew the word was for me. My heart raced as I moved forward with Natalie. I told the first worker that I saw that Natalie was the baby in question. I was immediately surrounded by seven or eight ministers who began to pray over us in tongues, and with great power.

When the prophet saw me, he said, "Get on one knee!" and I did so. "God says, 'You are going to be great in My name!'" The prophet continued, "Hundreds of thousands will come to Christ because of the work that the Lord will do through you!"

Then, more tongues went forth, and the interpretations of tongues. I was blessed and dazed for weeks after that, having never experienced anything like it. It was confirmation that I was not the only one experiencing the supernatural moves of God.

That night the Lord gave me my walking papers. I was confirmed as an evangelist with orders to travel everywhere, to preach the Gospel. It was time for me to set up shop near the gates of hell and go where angels feared to tread.

That next day I went to my regular church and, as I was leaving, I walked past a guy in the lobby with whom I went to school. It was my old friend, Wayne Fields, a former football player, and I had not seen him in twenty years! We looked back at the same time and burst into happy hugs and hand-shakes. We were talking for only a minute whereupon Wayne suddenly gave me the same prophecy that I received the night before at the Convention Center. When I told him about it, Wayne became extremely excited. He hugged me, jumped up and down and said, "God never used me prophetically before, or in the spiritual gifts!" He kept saying, "God's gonna' use you! God's gonna' use you!"

Shortly thereafter, I visited Messiah Christian Center in Los Angeles one Sunday morning, wherein the gifts of the Holy Spirit began to move once again. Pastor Kenneth Lamor Green pointed at me and before all said, "We have a great evangelist with us this morning." Then addressing me directly, "God has put healing in your hands."

Had I walked by seconds earlier or later, I would have never seen my old friend Wayne Fields, but the God Clock swings like a pendulum in the universe, with eternal precision. The Lord confirms His word with signs following. Natalie lived and did not die. She went on to attend medical school. Today, she is a registered nurse working with patients that have the same medical problems she had. Amen. That's what it's all about; helping each other. Only what we do for Christ will remain.

In 1990, I was leaving my house one day in a big hurry when it happened. God spoke right into my gut and it stopped me on the spot. The Lord said, "Call your Uncle Neal." So I ran back in the house to call him. Uncle Neal and I were very close, spiritually, and he was my favorite uncle. So I dialed his number and he answered right away. He said, "I've been trying to find you!"

There were no cell phones back in 1990, unless you paid a $500 deposit and went through a credit check. That's how rare they were back then, not to mention, they weighed about eight pounds and were the size of a brick.

"I've been trying to find you! We want you to come over to your Uncle L.J.'s house. He just got out of the hospital, so we can have prayer!"

When I arrived at Uncle L.J.'s house, four of my uncles and two cousins were there as well. Uncle L.J. just had surgery on his lungs and I had to get up close to him just to hear what he was saying.

In a whisper he said, "I heard you've been preaching."

"Yes, that's right." Then I asked him the question, "Have you received the Lord as personal savior?"

He said, "No."

"Would you like to receive the Lord now?"

He replied "Yes."

Amen! I led him to the Lord that day, along with two other uncles. About a month later, Uncle L.J. died. Two months later, his brother died who accepted the Lord that day died as well. The God Clock swings the pendulum of salvation, seeking whomever it may rescue at precisely the right time. Praise the Lord! I give Him all the glory for His love, rescue and timing. Go and be a blessing today in someone's life. God sees you and will reward you openly.

There was a time when I handed out 'Jesus t-shirts' to people on the street who received the Lord as their personal savior. During that time, the Lord put it on my heart to find a friend of mine. It was the crazy cat from the freeway shooting. Right after the shooting, the authorities picked him up and admitted him into the Metro Mental Facility, where he remained for observation for thirty days. A tall, good-looking man with long, fly' hair, he was often the target of jealousy. Someone put a hit on him, shot him five times, and he survived. Unlike me, he had no pillar of fire to protect him.

I helped him during his convalescence until he got better but he continued in his dangerous consumption of angel dust, heroin and cocaine. It was now 1989 and the day came when the Lord pressed it on my heart to go and find him. In fact, the Lord would not let it go and kept this guy on my heart and mind continually. When I finally found him, he was exceedingly glad to see me. I shared the word of God with him, and seeing the changes in my own life, he broke down and cried like a baby. We prayed together that day and he received the Lord. He said, "Yes, I do believe!"

I gave him a Jesus t-shirt. He took off his own shirt and put it on right away. Then I dropped him off at his apartment. That next morning, his girlfriend called to tell me that he had died in his sleep. Praise the Lord. God is the beginning and the end. Man is appointed once to die, then comes the judgment. The God Clock rescued my friend who was scheduled for hell in but a few short hours. My funny, crazy, good-looking, beloved friend now walks the Streets of Paradise, resting safely in the bosom of Jesus.

Although the God Clock ticks in the universe like a pendulum, many don't accept the invitation. For those, time sadly runs out. Take for instance another old friend who I ran into one day. I had not seen him in a long time and when he saw me again, I was a Christian. Even his close friends said, "Don't let him corrupt you!"

By now I had my Christian values together and was walking uprightly before the Lord. He was also raised as a Christian but all of us are different. Even his daughters said, "I wish our Mom had met you first." One of his daughters said, "I believe my Dad is going to get real sick very soon and I will be the one stuck to take care of him." Such was his out-of-control lifestyle.

One of his friends had lots of money and they spoke often about me. "Bruce was not like this before. He used to sell drugs and was a pimp, making lots of money."

So his friend, who had four homes in Palos Verdes worth three to four million each, actually asked me if I still had any drug connections. So I told him that I've been out of the game for a long time, but he offered me $100,000 for just one connection. Of course, I declined, but he persisted.

"Well, let me give you the money now and you can think about it for a week." He tried to coerce me this way over the next four months.

"Hey, it's on me, not you," he would say. "No really, here take it!"

The devil will do just about anything to get you back, even if it means pushing a hundred large into your chest, pressed down, shaken together and running over.

I said, "No!" for the last time.

My friend who introduced me to this rich man was just as bad. He invited me to all these functions, as they still liked having me around so I went. You have to understand that the evangelist dares to get closer to the gates of hell than any other church office. Many times the evangelist's hair and clothes become singed, if that's what it takes to pull people from the flames of eternal torment.

And so I went to their parties and worldly functions robed in the anointing as the Ambassador of Christ, praying for people and sharing the Word of God. My friend stood back in the distance with his drinking buddies, watching on as I prayed and preached with the other party guests. They raised their glasses, amused from across the room, calling out, "There goes Bruce trying to save the world," to which I responded, "You got that right!"

The Bible declares, "Death and life are in the power of the tongue," ... "Touch not My anointed," and, "Do my prophets no harm."

The millionaire who kept trying to bribe me with $100,000 eventually committed suicide, and my friend who introduced me to him was attacked with cancer. I called him one day and he could hardly speak. He whispered, "Call me tomorrow," but he died the next day.

Chapter 10

Drinking New Wine ...

At the Liquor Store!

As mentioned earlier, by 1989 I was fully immersed in the Lord. No longer was I in the infantile stages, where just anything could come along and attack me, nor was I ignorant as to the will of God. I had come a long way since 1975, when I walked naked down the street, wrapped in a sheet.

I took proactive steps to draw closer to God as He had done toward me. I prayed daily, read my Bible and actually fasted every now and then. One day, a friend of mine told me about a part-time job at a certain liquor store. For years I had gone downtown, to Los Angeles's skid row, bringing the destitute food and clothing, and I knew the liquor store all too well. I told him, "No, I'm not working at a liquor store!" By then, such jobs were against my beliefs. He replied, "Well, you're always helping people and it will mean more money for you!" But I said again, "I'm not working in a liquor store and that's final!"

Shortly thereafter, I began a fast. On the fourth day into the fast, I was driving home and when I arrived, I attempted to get out of the car. As my foot touched the ground, it was as though I had stepped on fire. The fire, raging beneath my foot wasn't an audible voice, but a fire burning actual instructions into my being. The interpretation came just as quickly. I was to go to the liquor store in question, apply for a job, and 'work' there. The words of fire were, "I'm going to use you at that liquor store." It was a divine order and I was to go there as a messenger. So I went there, met with the owner and took the interview.

A woman, whom I believed was his wife, was there at the time and she was very much pregnant; as though she were due any minute. He told her to take me into the back of the liquor store and tell me about the job. I asked her how long they had been married, and she said,

"We're not married. You don't have to be married to have a child," and I agreed. I ministered so much love to her about God, her maker, and what is right in His sight. Long story short, I got the job working at the liquor store.

I worked there for about two months, during which time, many supernatural things occurred, with respect to people receiving Christ into their lives. The church I attended at the time circulated printed invitations. The owner allowed me to put some on the counter, so that whenever customers purchased something, I gave them an invitation to come to church. People might say, "What?! In a liquor store?!" but the word of God states, "Behold, I send you forth as sheep in the midst of wolves. Therefore, be wise as serpents and harmless as doves. Go out and find the lost sheep and bring them home."

When Jesus chose the disciples, they were fisherman; crude, smelly, uneducated. And yet in the span of three short years, they became transformed into His image. Oh yeah sure, some, like Peter and Judas, stumbled very badly, but God never withdrew His hand of outreach toward them. In fact, upon Christ's resurrection, He charged the twelve remaining disciples with the greatest commission of all--to evangelize the world! "Go now and catch all men." The call on my life and the Father's faithfulness directed me to that liquor store.

A man walked in one day with his son and exclaimed, "How are you?!"

I replied, "I'm blessed!"

He said, "Hey, I *know* who you are!"

"You talk like you know me," I replied.

He said, "Yeah, I do."

As I returned his change, I looked at him with a question mark on my face and said, "Well, I give up. I don't know who you are." He went on to tell me about one faithful night years earlier.

"Four years ago, I was sitting on the corner of 54th and Vermont in Los Angeles, hungry and destitute. You bought me dinner, prayed for me, gave me some money. And I never forgot you."

His son was with him that day at the liquor store and both seemed to be doing well. He was very thankful and the Lord let me know that my work back then was not in vain. That was truly a blessing. So many wonderful things happened in that liquor store. The area was a stroll for prostitution, and yet, these working girls respected the call on my life. For one thing, they stopped saying flirtatious things whenever they saw me. God actually amplified their voices as they talked about me way down the street, and many times I heard their conversations from inside the store. I listened as they said things like, "Don't say stuff like that about Bruce, unless you're ready to get right with God!"

One day, an older man with a little hat on his head came into the liquor store and bought a hot-dog and a half-pint of wine. When he paid for the products, I said, "Have a blessed day." He stopped in his tracks and said, "Are you a *Christian*?"

"Yes."

"In a *liquor* store?!" he asked excitedly. Then he scratched his head and left. About twenty minutes later, he came back in and continued with the same questions, as if he had never left.

"Okay, so you mean to tell me that you're a *Christian*?!"

"Yes! Why, what's wrong?" I smiled. "Don't you believe in God?"

"Well, my wife has been trying to get me to go to church with her for a long time..."

"Well, that's why God sent me here...to encourage you to go. Don't you believe in God?"

He said, "Yes, but..."

"Well, go to church with your wife...it's okay!"

"So... you're a *Christian?!*"

Then the little man left, still scratching his head. It was almost comical. I didn't see him again for a few days after that, but in my heart I knew God moved on his life, just from the look in his eyes, as he kept asking me over and over, "So, you're a *Christian*?!"

The Lord showed me that what he needed was for someone to stand boldly and unabashed for the Lord, and tell him to go to church with his wife. In fact, a few people I met at the store started going to church with me. Amen. Only God truly knows what people need.

One night I stopped at *another* liquor store across town, not to buy liquor but just to pick up a few supplies. Standing ominously right in front of the store was a big, intimidating man, asking people for money. I believe the people working there were afraid of him because they didn't tell him to move. As I approached the door, he asked me for money too, so I said, "I'll talk to you when I come back."

On my way out, I addressed him and said, "Okay, so let me talk to you for a minute," and he followed behind me. I started the interaction by asking the man, "Are you trying to scare people because you're a big guy? First of all, I'm a Christian. I once was a player and a hustler, so I know the game. And now, I serve God. I'm a street evangelist." I told him my name and he told me his.

I said, "Good to meet you. So look, are you a good guy trying to be bad?" Then he smiled and I saw the mischievous twinkle in his eye. This opened the door and made him feel comfortable talking to me. He said he used to read his Bible all the time, and that he knew the word, but now he was a backslider.

I prayed with him and after the prayer, you should have seen the big smile on his face. This frightening-looking man was now a gentle giant. We talked for about an hour and this man changed right before my eyes. The Lord had me spend quality time with him because everyone needs a friend or someone they can trust at one time or another.

He knew many of the people hanging out on the street corner and he called them over with a loud voice, saying "Come over here so this man can pray for you!"

We had church right there in the parking lot of the liquor store. Several young men prayed for salvation that night and received the Lord. I drive by that area periodically and whenever he saw me, he lit up with a big smile. I had made a good friend, one that will be going to Paradise with me.

Meantime, back at the liquor store where I worked, a real sharp-looking Mercedes pulled up and a well-dressed, young man walked in, wearing lots of jewelry, looking tailored to the max. As discussed earlier, I kept invitations to church on the counter. After he purchased his liquor, I spoke to him about the Lord and going to church.

"I used to go to church with my grandmother," he said introspectively, whereupon I gave him the flyer and invited him to come to church, but he didn't take it. I continued to minister to him and he said, "Man, you're scaring me," and he started to back out of the store. I called out after him, "The Lord is calling you to get right today! You might not have another chance!"

Then he left and one hour later, I saw him drive up to the liquor store again. He got out of the car, walked in weeping, and asked for that invitation to church. I gladly gave it to him and he said, "I *know* I need to get right with God!"

Praise the Lord! That was a powerful moment to witness! God draws us to Him at an appointed time. He never gives up on us.

On yet another night, I'm working at the liquor store when two ladies walked in wearing Jesus pins. With excitement I said, "My sisters in the Lord!"

With an ugly attitude they replied, "What do you mean sisters in the Lord? You're in a liquor store!"

I could have said the same thing about them being there, but I didn't. I merely preached a quick sermonette to them, on how the Lord said to go out into all the world, preach the Gospel to the lost sheep and bring them home.

"We are to let God's people know that this is a love walk!"

Then, they repented on the spot. They apologized and said, "Brother, we didn't know you were *walking* like that."

Church people can be their own worst enemies. Just remember: you will know the true Christians by their fruit; in other words, their behavior.

Right on the corner was Victory Outreach, a well-known, Los Angeles street-outreach church. One day, five pastors from Victory walked into the store and said, "Are you Brother Bruce?" I said yes.

"We heard the Lord sent you here. We're praying for you!"

The Lord said, "Go into all the world and preach the Gospel to every creature." Yep, even at the liquor store.

Chapter 11

The Genesis Gym

The awesome thing about God is that we can work for him in a business suit or smelly tennis shoes. And it just so happens that my local gym proved to be the genesis rising of many transformed lives.

One day, I was at the local gym in the sauna, sharing the word of God with someone. That one left and this other guy sitting about five feet away moved closer to me and asked if I was I talking about God? I said yes. I asked if he was a believer, he said he wasn't sure.

I said, "What do you mean?"

"Well, I was raised to believe there was no God."

"Well, that's not true. God is real."

He replied, "I'm beginning to feel that's true because I'm meeting a lot of Christians lately."

I pointed out, "God must have something in store for you because he is drawing you. The Bible says, 'The Spirit of God draws all men unto Him.'" Then I switched gears and suggested we step out of the sauna for a minute.

"Let's see what's on your heart."

He asked, "Can God help me?"

I said, "He sure can. He made you!"

"But my Dad always told me that there is no God."

"Well, there is. Do you have a Bible?"

He said, "No, but I can buy one."

I asked, "What kind of work do you do?"

"I'm a proof reader for Warner Brothers Studio."

"Okay, so you read all the time! Do you mind if I pray for you right now? Is there a certain thing you want God to do?"

"Yes. I can't stop drinking.

"Wow!" I exclaimed. "You don't even *look* like you drink!"

"I know, but I drink every day."

"Okay, well let me have this prayer with you."

So I prayed for him and then instructed him to read the Gospel of John, Chapter 1.

"In the beginning was the word…I want you to start talking to what you *cannot see* and say, 'Lord help me, show me,' or however you want to say it. God understands."

About two weeks later, I went back to the local gym and all of a sudden, someone shouted my name very loudly with great excitement from across the room.

"Hey Bruce!...Bruce!...I think I got it!"

I turned around and saw the same guy I prayed with about his drinking problem. I knew then that God had moved upon him. He came over to me, shook my hand and gave me a hug.

He said, "I did everything you instructed. I bought the Bible, read the whole chapter of John and prayed, but then I took a drink, anyway. Only this time, I got really sick and kept throwing up all over my house. That was two weeks ago."

I saw him again three years ago, and he had not taken a drink in all that time. God instantly moved on his life. The Bible declares, "No one knows the heart but God." God knows our hearts and He knew the sincerity of that man's heart. He is the maker of life and knows us better than we know ourselves. He's not a respecter of persons, like humans are. In other words, He has no favorites and gives love and rescue to all, equally and liberally.

Now, I usually work out four to five days a week whenever I have time, but this particular day was different. In my belly, I felt compelled to go to the gym immediately. I looked at the time and the gym was going to close in one hour, but I could not shake the feeling, so I grabbed my stuff and went.

When I walked into the gym, I saw this one guy who was a regular at the gym. He is a big man, about six-feet, five inches in height. He was talking quite loudly, actually, to a young man about the girl he was dating.

"Man, are you not hittin' that?" to which the young man replied, "Sex is not everything. I like her! She's a good person."

When the big man saw me enter the work-out room he looked over at me and called out, "Hey man, shouldn't he be hittin' that stuff?"

I asked the big man for his name, which is Ron, and he was about to collide with his maker. "Well, Big Ron, a few years back, I would have agreed with you, but now I serve God. I'm a Christian." Just then I felt the evil flee from the room. When I said that, his head fell to his chest and he became very quiet for a moment. I asked, "What's wrong?"

"I'm a backslider. I once spoke just like you."

I said, "Ron, this is your day to come home. You can repent and I will pray with you right now."

I prayed with Big Ron right there in the work-out room before God and man, and he was very thankful. Then I went to another area in the gym, and Ron walked in with a big smile on his face when he saw me. A while later, I walked over to another workout area; a large two-story room on the other side of the gym. The facility is huge and there's no way that Ron could have known where I went each time.

A little while later, he again walked into the same room I was in. He didn't expect to run into me again and neither did I. So when he saw me, he threw up his hands in resignation and shouted with a loud voice, "His angels are encamped all around me!" It was his humorous response to us bumping into each other again and again. We laughed and he threw up his hands praising God.

What an awesome God we serve. He never forgets us, even in our worst state. God saw Big Ron at the gym that day and yearned for him to come home. So He rustled me out of my comfort zone and compelled me to go and get him; thereby reminding me that I work for Him.

My Father God does not fail. The Bible states, "His ways are not our ways; His thoughts are not our thoughts."

On yet another occasion, I was at the gym enjoying the bubbly waters of the Jacuzzi when an attractive, young lady walked in and sat on the opposite side in the water. I saw her there a few times before but never actually talked to her. This day, however, was different. The Lord put it into my heart to share His word with her and we sat in the Jacuzzi together.

So I approached her and asked, "Mind if I sit here? I'd like to share something with you. She said, "Okay."

I learned that she was a believer, but was a little down that day. The Lord sent me to encourage her, and realizing this, tears came to her eyes. She said, "Thank you."

As I walked away, she called me and said, "Wait!" As she stepped out of the Jacuzzi, she asked if she could give me a hug, with tears still in her eyes. I said, "Sure!"

As I walked away, two guys came up to me and asked, "What did you say to her? We've been trying to talk to her for *weeks*, but she won't speak to anyone! What did you say?"

I told them that I spoke to her about God. You should have seen their faces; totally confused, like "What?" And then I walked away. I knew it was their day to seek Him.

God knows what to do to get our attention. Those young men will never forget the incident. That's why they were watching. If fact, you just never know who's watching you!

Chapter 12

Miracles at the Marketplace

I went to the burger stand one evening located around the corner from my apartment and a man walked up to me asking for money. He said he was trying to buy some liquor. It was quite honest of him to come right out and say so. Usually, they'll tell you they need 'bus fare' or 'gas money.' Next thing you know, they can be seen going into the nearest liquor store to 'buy gas.' They're all poor souls with such strong addictions, they actually think we don't know what they do with the money.

So I shared with him my past lifestyle and how I used to drink, and he actually listened intently. Then he asked me, "What made you quit?"

I shared my testimony with him. He was very interested and asked many engaging questions. God moved on him quite rapidly. His heart was opened to receive and he did. Suddenly, a second guy walked up like the first one had, also asking for "money to buy liquor." The first guy started laughing and said, "Hey man, I did the same thing you just did; that's why I'm laughin.' You need to hear this man's testimony, how God *saved* him!"

So now, God moved on the first guy, and I stepped back for a minute, watching God use him so quickly. It was the domino effect. I watched on as the first man ministered to the second man. God partners up with us and picks up the heavy load, if only we let Him.

One day, I traveled up to Northern California to help my cousin run his twenty-four hour *7-11 Convenience Store* for a while. My cousin is also a Christian and when I arrived, he told me about a man who came into the store, late every night, known as Old Man Joe. Now, this particular *7-11* had seats and tables in the back of the store where people could sit and have coffee.

"He comes in every night, buys the paper, and sits over there in the corner reading the whole thing," described my cousin. "He's an older man with lots of money, but he dresses like a bum. Everyone knows him as Old Man Joe. He's got an old, beat-up truck and he's not a believer." My cousin continued, "Apparently, the old man loaned a few businesses in the area some money, so he's not poor. I never pushed God on him, but while he sits there reading the paper, he observes me talking to customers about the Lord, and he listens in on the conversations."

As soon as I started working at the *7-11*, sure enough, Old Man Joe came in every night and did everything my cousin described. After several weeks of watching us witness to customers, the old man finally spoke to me and with a mischievous twinkle in his eye he said, "Hey Bruce! Do *you* believe in God?"

He knew that I did. I just smiled and so did he. In all that time, he spoke perhaps five or six words to us, and then came the breakthrough. After a few weeks of this routine, he walked in as usual, only this time he *shouted* my name!

"Hey, Bruce!"

Old Man Joe held up a Bible he brought into the store to read. Amen! He was a man of few words, and yet that night, he said it all. The Lord had won his heart, through the example of our testimony.

Another time I went to a water store that was owned by a Christian husband and wife, a friendly couple. They said business had been slow so I prayed with them for a financial breakthrough. By then I had recorded my testimonial CDs and gave them one. They shared it with their family and all of them loved it!

Whenever I went to their store, I noticed the wife was always smoking cigarettes outside the store, and I said to myself, *Next time we talk, I will ask if she wants prayer to stop smoking cigarettes.*

About two weeks later, I went into the store to say 'hello' and when I drove up she was smoking cigarettes outside again. The couple was happy to see me. Then I asked if there was anything they would like prayer about, and the wife said, "We've been trying to get pregnant for nineteen years."

Just then, I felt God's presence very strongly as we stood there talking. Now was the perfect time to tell her what the Lord laid on my heart.

"First, you need to quit smoking." She agreed, so I prayed for her to immediately stop smoking, in the name of Jesus. Then I prayed for God to open her womb in order to conceive a baby in the name of Jesus. The presence and peace of God was thick and tangible in the store that day.

Well, she got pregnant that very next month. They called me right after they learned of the news and today they have a baby boy! Amen. It's never too late for God when you believe. The Lord proved to them that He exists and it was through this miracle that their walk with the Lord deepened.

Sometimes you can talk to people about the Lord until you're blue in the face and they will never reach out to Him...until, they receive a miracle, that is. For it is by miracles that our God distinguishes Himself apart from all other gods who are dead and cannot heal a thing!

I once knew a doctor that I liked and we were good friends, but he was involved in a religion that I did didn't agree with. It also seemed that he could not talk about anything with a positive attitude. I stopped by his office one day and dropped off my testimonial CD. About a week later, he called and asked me to bring more CDs. When I walked in, he had a serious look on his face, and smiling, I said, "What's up, doc?"

He said, "Okay, so, I listened to your CD and you spoke about demons that you've seen. Well, the other day after a patient left my office, there was a terrible smell in the air, a really terrible odor, and I could hardly breathe. Then, in a cloud-like mist, a demon appeared and stood in front of my desk. This thing was horrible-looking, all dark and hairy. Then, another one appeared that was white and hairy, and they made these frightening sounds! Then, a third demon appeared and this one was a nine-foot dragon with fire coming out of its nose and mouth, saying "I'm going to take you to hell!"

The demon said this to him right there in his office! He knew that his own, strange religion could never protect him from such demonic attacks. I know these experiences changed his whole life. I prayed with him that day and he still calls me periodically for prayer.

Miracles in the marketplace continued. One day I was out and about with my Christian friends, and I was having a *really* bad day after a series of adverse events. In fact, I told them, "God doesn't love me!" I was quite upset and actually walked away from them.

Later that night, I went shopping with my lady-friend and while at the cash register, I saw an opportunity to witness to the owner of the store about the Lord, so I did. This brought tears to her eyes and she asked me to wait a moment and not leave. As we waited for her, I felt a light tapping on my leg. I turned around and saw a little girl, about four to five years old. As I looked down at her, she said, "God loves you."

Then her mother walked up and I told her what her little girl had just said, which greatly startled her.

"What? My baby can't even talk!"

It turns out that her little girl had been mute since birth but the Lord spoke through her mouth in answer to the nonsense I spoke earlier that day. ("God doesn't love me," if you recall.)

God will speak through *anyone* to let us know how much He loves us, even if that little vessel was a deaf-mute all her life!

On another occasion, I drove into a gas station and instantly a horde of men came running toward me, wanting to pump my gas in exchange for loose change. It was obvious that all fifteen were crack-heads on cocaine, dirty and living on the street.

Watching this onslaught of wounded flesh coming toward me I knew how Jesus felt when the group of lepers accosted Him. The Spirit of the Lord came upon me at that moment and with my hands lifted up, I called out with a loud voice, "In the name of Jesus, hold each other's hands and let me pray for your salvation!"

I said, "Cry out to the Lord right now to save you!"

These young men got around my car, holding hands, crying and repeating, "Help me Lord! Help me Lord!"

I watched as the awesome, amazing miracle unfolded before my very eyes. It was like watching the parting of the Sea of Moses, only their souls were being parted to make way for the coming of the Lord.

At this appointed time, I was promoting a play entitled, *Tell Hell I Ain't Comin.'* I gave some of the guys flyers to pass out for a few days and paid them for their services to show them that I cared.

For centuries, people have been taught 'by the church' that God condemns us into repentance, and that He 'teaches us' things through chastisement. That's a complete fabrication! The Apostle Paul stated in Romans 2:4, "For it is God's KINDNESS that leads us to repentance!"

Chapter 13

The
In-Your-Face Anointing

One night in 1986, Smokey Robinson made the mistake of walking into *Ablaze Ministry*, located on West Florence Avenue, in downtown Los Angeles. Dr. Jean Perez was the resident prophet there; a charismatic woman filled with the Holy Ghost, from which nothing and no one could hide a thing.

She called Smokey to the front for prayer, whereupon he was healed of his addiction to crack-cocaine, having never touched another drug since then. Jean Perez has the in-your-face anointing. It cannot be argued with, negotiated, bargained with or escaped.

Another way of saying 'in your face' is 'well-documented.' Jean is a very good friend of mine, so she called me one day to come and visit her church for the specific purpose of performing a healing. She said, "Brother Bruce, come and agree with me for a young lady's leg. The one leg is almost twelve inches shorter than the other!"

When we arrived at the church, about fifty people were in attendance. We sought out the young lady during the service, gathered around her and began to pray. As soon as we stretched forth our hands, right before our very eyes, the shorter leg grew out very quickly, about a *foot longer* than the normal leg! Then it evened up with the normal leg until both were the same length!

God moved instantly because He's an 'instant God.' He said, "Let there be light!" and light came instantly. He created the rest of the universe in the same way, instantly. He graciously extended the same benefit to us when He said, "Before you call, I answer!" It all depends on what we can believe for. Therefore, let us exercise our faith daily so that we can receive instantly when real trouble comes. See, that's the missing ingredient: believing for small things daily, so that we can believe for monumental things as they arise. Believe God for a postage stamp or a free cup of coffee on one day. The day after that, believe Him for extra fuel in your car, or a good parking spot at the restaurant. Make a point of increasing your faith and work your way up from there. Faith is a daily exercise, an adventure!

When people ran up to Jesus for help, He questioned them specifically to locate their level of faith. He asked them, "What can you believe? What do you want Me to do for you? Do you believe that I can do this?"

God confirms His word with signs following. After that, the young lady's entire family started going to church once they saw her new leg. How could they not in view of such an in-your-face miracle, knowing she had been crippled all her life?

But wait, there's more! I gave one of my testimonial CDs to a new friend, a young lady with a ten-year old daughter. The little girl had a pet hamster to which she was very emotionally attached. The young mother went to pick up the little girl from school one day while playing my CD in the car and as they listened I spoke about all the miracles the Lord performed through my hands during my walk with Him. Then, the CD came to the part where I spoke about having died twice, and how the Lord brought me back to life. The little girl loved this part of the story, and it would prove to play a significant role in her young life very shortly.

In fact, the little girl wanted to meet me so for starters, I spoke with her over the phone. It's quite possible that the little girl has a prophetic calling of miracles resting upon her own life, since children usually react to anything fragrant of their own destiny.

That next week, her hamster died. The little girl was beside herself; she cried and would not be comforted. Her mother put the hamster in a shoe box and gently buried the little, furry thing in the backyard, but this was not enough for the little girl. She had faith the size of a sky-scraper!

She cried, "Mommy, let's pray like the man did on the CD!"

Her mother knew the hamster had already been dead for twenty-four hours and rigor mortis had consumed the animal's body beyond repair; but she obliged the child, anyway. As mother and daughter prayed for the little hamster to come back to life, suddenly the box began to shake and rattle!

Wouldn't you know it? The hamster came back to life! We should all practice this kind of child-like, persistent faith, remembering that if God has done this for others, we also are entitled.

Well, they could hardly wait to call me. God is good. That little girl and her mother will now use this incident as a monument of their faith, which they will refer back to over and over for the rest of their lives. If the Lord will heal a simple hamster, what won't He do for us?

On a less happy note, the Christian church conceals many poor representatives who proclaim to be sent by God, and clearly they are not. It is at such times that the in-your-face anointing steps in to keep the Body of Christ accountable. God is only love and wholesomeness, and yet in many ministers standing at the pulpit, there is only debauchery and deceit. We can easily identify them by their behavior, but the question is: should we turn a blind eye? On the contrary; the Apostle Paul instructed us to expose them without partiality–no matter who they are, or how famous.

I was invited to a certain church one day and listened to the particular pastor speaking. He knew the word of God quite well, spoke very eloquently and riveted the congregation into crescendo and decrescendo; but there was just something not right about this man, something that just didn't sit right with me. After the service, I met up with him and mentioned conferencing with him some time in near the future. In preparation for this, I fasted four days, because I wanted answers.

One week later, I approached him after the service and asked if he had a minute to talk. He said, "Sure." There were a lot of ladies hovering and gushing over him. "Excuse me ladies," he crooned, as any good playa' would, which I knew he was. In fact, he was so good at his game; he might have worked for me back in the day.

When the ladies left, I said, "Pastor, I asked God about you. I said, 'Lord, is this man of you?'"

Stunned, he said, "Brother, give me a minute," and he took off. When he came back, he looked me straight in the eyes, dropped his head and said, "I can't talk to you; I can't *ever* talk to you!" Then he walked backwards out of his own church. "I won't *ever* be able to talk to you!"

As I stood there, watching this man back all the way out the door, God gave me the answer I sought. He was not of God and the in-your-face anointing had exposed him. Later on, I heard he was arrested at the church for inappropriately touching a teenager on her breast. He also cheated several people out of their money.

I thank God for using me as I yield myself to the Father. May this book be a blessing to those who depend on God, not man. Go to the Father yourself. Since the crucifixion, we have been granted autonomy and don't need anyone else, like a priest, to stand before God on our behalf. We can go before Him on our own as the beloved sons and daughters of the Living God. Ask him to guide and direct you by His Spirit of Truth that was promised to us by our Lord and Savior, Jesus Christ.

On yet another occasion, I was invited to a meeting conducted inside a home one evening. The home was a nice, large, two-story structure and about sixty people showed up. The home-service was conducted by the pastor who also owned a separate, church building.

The pastor invited a guest speaker to lead the meeting that night while he went upstairs for a moment to his study. Well, it didn't take long for me to stand up in front of everyone and rebuke the guest speaker because of the utter garbage he was preaching. He peddled the old, worn-out lie that we should never speak against a pastor, "No matter what he does!" whereupon he proceeded to run a shopping list of sinful behaviors that any given minister might be engaged in, and that we better not say anything about it.

This line of doctrine is broad, sweeping and dangerous, and left to one's untrained interpretation leaves us wide open for destruction. For instance, what if a pastor is engaged in secret sin with another man's wife? What if he coerced his congregation into an investment scheme and spent the money on himself? We certainly *do not* have to be quiet about such behaviors and the Apostle Paul gave us explicit instructions concerning this in 1st Timothy 5:19-21. Take a look:

> Those [elders] who are sinning rebuke in the presence of all, so that all may fear. I charge you before God and the Lord Jesus Christ...that you observe these things without prejudice, doing nothing with partiality.

Just as I rebuked the guest speaker, the pastor came down the stairs and asked, "What just happened?" So I told him about the false teaching that the guest speaker was attempting to peddle and I reminded the pastor, "This isn't God! Are you aware of what he's preaching?"

The pastor responded, "Well, let's give him another chance," so I did; but the damage was done. After that, the guest speaker really couldn't get it together so he asked me to share a message, and I did.

Many in the church believe that the, 'Touch Not My Anointed' message applies also to deceivers and charlatans, but it does not. It applies only to those ministers who live uprightly before the Lord. (Touch them, and you better run for cover.)

The Holy Spirit really moved in the meeting after that. The guests stood in front of me for prayer, so I prayed, laying hands on them, in the name of Jesus, and people were getting set free. Then, a lady brought up her daughter and asked me to pray for her. She was probably around fifteen years old at the time and the daughter received the prayer.

However, there was another teenage girl there who would not stand up and engage. So, I gently addressed the young girl, and said, "In the name of Jesus, stand up!" Just then, a demon manifested itself and said, "No!" It was a man's voice, not a young girl's. Because of the in-your-face anointing, the demon was exposed. I laid hands on her and commanded the demon to come out.

"In Jesus' name, come out of her!" But she leaped about six feet into the hallway. Then, this un-anointed pastor walked up to her, because he knew the girl, called her by name and started hugging and comforting the girl.

"There, there; it's okay, it's okay."

Little did he know that he was actually comforting the demon who still had not been reckoned with. In effect, he babied the demon and allowed it to incubate inside the girl. Who knew what utter chaos it would drive her into later in life; crime, prostitution, murder, prison, a fatal disease? It was only a matter of time.

I never went back to that congregation. Lots of people left after that. They sought me out for prayer whenever they saw me, but it was not me they sought, it was Christ. Perhaps they had never experienced the Lord's presence at this church. How can a man of God preaching God's word not rebuke a demon?

The in-your-face anointing cannot be argued with, negotiated, bargained with or escaped.

Chapter 14

Cookin' With Christ

I'm a cook and owned several restaurants over the years. My first was the *Mr. Goodburger*, home of the best hamburgers in town, on West Vernon Avenue in Los Angeles. After that I partnered up with the *Super Scoop Restaurants* and cooked for them outside, patio style. *Super Scoop #1* was located on 61st and Atlantic Avenue, while the *Super Scoop #2* was on 68th and Cherry Avenue; both in sunny Long Beach; or more affectionately, the *LBC*.

A friend of mine told a certain production company about my chefly talents and shortly after that I received a phone call from one of the producers. They were looking for a cook to go on location while shooting a movie. Not only did they need a cook, but they heard I was a *great cook!* Anybody hungry? (smile)

My spiritual calling is that of a street evangelist so I share the word of God with everyone I meet, feeding them with good, *spiritual* food and *real* food. People listen better on a full stomach, and only a true evangelist will ever know that. In fact, all the downtown missions might want to try this new approach if they really want to get through to people on skid-row. Instead of starving them into hearing the Gospel, try feeding them first. You'd be surprised how many of these street urchins would actually stay and listen.

There were quite a few rappers on the movie set. I talked with them, shared the word of God and they were actually quite interested in my background as a former pimp, and the fact that I was now a street preacher. I also told them about demons and my experience with the supernatural.

Before long, one of the guys pulled me to the side and said, "I need to talk to you alone." Later, he told me that he had been seeing a beautiful, young lady and often spent the night at her house. Now, every time he lay in her bed, she would be fast asleep next to him, while he up listening to these other-worldly footsteps stomping about all over her house and up in the ceiling. She lived alone so there was no one else in the house. Each time it happened, he told her about it the next day but she just shrugged it off.

"Oh that; it's nothing, don't worry about it."

Foolishly, her beauty kept him coming back but then he stopped going to her house all together because he couldn't take it anymore, but now it seemed the phantom footsteps followed him to his own house! By then, he heard me talk about Jesus on the production set and my simple message turned out to save his life.

One night he was lying on his bed about to go to sleep and a powerful force pushed him down into the bed, if trying to crush him through the mattress. The man said it felt like he was going to die. He started shouting out loud, "Jesus help! Jesus help!" over and over for few several minutes. Then it left and never come back. Make no mistake; it was the name of Jesus that rescued him that night. Calling on that name is the reason he is still alive today.

I soon returned to the *Super Scoop 1 & 2* patios. Some of the patrons called me 'The Cooking Preacher.' Cooking outside was great because everyone sees you as they walk or drive by, and everyone gets to know you.

Now, whenever I worked at the *Super Scoop #2*, a certain young lady walked by every day taking her little girl to school and she dressed very provocatively. Cars blew their horns and men whistled and hollered out the window whenever she walked down the street. Witnessing all this, I knew she loved the attention. In fact, she walked by all the time, smiled at me, saying, "Hello."

I noticed she had a tattoo on her leg. I couldn't see what it said, so one day I asked her about it and she answered, "100% Bitch." She laughed and kept walking. Right after that, the Lord said, "Pray for her." She stayed in my spirit for two weeks, so when I saw her again, I said, "I need to tell you something." So she came over to me and I told her that God loves her and has plans for her life.

"There will be some positive changes from this point forward. I've been praying for you." She replied with tears in her eyes, "Now, I have something to look forward to."

People are waiting for us to show them God's love!

Chapter 15

God Loves Pedophiles!

In 1998, I was hired by a lady who owned a dozen properties around Los Angeles, wherein she provided home-care for invalids and disturbed persons; among them pedophiles. It's a well-known fact that they cannot be rehabilitated, but for the vice-breaking power of Christ.

When I started at the facility, I reviewed each patient's record and realized that half of them were pedophiles. In fact, the owner of the facility was the only person in the State of California to actually take in convicted pedophiles. There were six to eight in the house where I was stationed and they were all diagnosed with 'mental illness.'

From the very first day of my employ at the house, they made it clear that I could not preach religion to the 'clients.' Now, I'm a street preacher. I embrace everyone no matter what they've done, but I determined right from the start not to break the house rules. God opened this door for a reason and he would no doubt rearrange things in His own way. He would get the glory no matter what happened next.

This was a live-in position at four days a week. I cooked, cleaned, passed out medications and attended to the patients' needs. No longer desiring to earn a living selling women and drugs at $80,000 a month, I was perfectly happy to settle into the kind of honest work where I could exercise my gifts and calling by doing what I enjoyed the most -- caring for people! And after getting paid a humble salary to boot, I was a happy, satisfied man.

Two attendants worked together each day on different assignments; two men and two women on different days. I had a room all to myself with twin beds. During my break time, I would eat lunch and read my Bible, which I did daily. I kept my door open to make sure I heard the commotion, should a situation arise.

And then one day, one of the ladies that worked there came into my room to introduce herself, so we talked for a few minutes. I was studying at the time so my Bible was open. Then, she started getting a little too comfortable and proceeded to lie down on the other bed. I told her this was my quite time but she didn't take the hint. Instead, she had the nerve to say, "I don't mind. I'll just lay here for a minute." She really got on my nerves.

So I bumped it up a notch and said, "You need to lie down in your own room. You're not supposed to be in here, anyway, so I would appreciate it if you would leave."

To this she reasoned, "Well, okay, but we do work together..." as if that gave us license for contraband. I replied, "Yes, but not in here. See you later."

Satan roams the Earth like a roaring lion seeking someone that he may devour, with emphasis on the word "may." He cannot help himself unless we give him permission, and he certainly didn't get it that day.

That next week the young lady and I were again working the same shift. I got up at 3:00 A.M. to use the restroom and walked down the hall toward the bathroom. The lights were still off in my room so upon my return I opened the door and saw something hideous; the large shadow of something loaded up on the other bed.

I blinked and opened the door wider so the light from the hallway flooded in and that's when I saw it...a big, black, naked butt in my room. It was the young lady in question. How did she get into my room within a matter of moments? Being still sleepy, I thought I was seeing things. So I got a better look and said out loud, "Oh my God!"

She didn't move or say anything, pretending to be asleep. That was against rules, so I went onto the restroom to think. When I returned she was gone. I waited a few days and told the director. The next time I saw the butt-bandit, she was an indignant, hot mess pretending to ignore me as the director took note of her behavior.

Now, I heard the owner was making over a $100,000 a month in revenue from all of her care facilities. One day, she asked me to go with her to make several bank deposits. As we drove along, a car suddenly pulled in front of us and almost caused an accident. At that moment she turned and looked at me in a most seductive way and said, "I can't let anything happen to *you*. I *know* you take care of your girls."

This turn of events surprised me. I didn't reply to anything she said as she so obviously flirted with me. Then it got quiet in the car for a minute, whereupon she said, "You must be a church man," but I remained silent. I was learning a lot about her and she kept putting her foot in her mouth.

Eventually I said, "I am a Christian, a minister and evangelist," and that's all she needed to know. We went to four different banks making deposits. As soon as I got this job, women were all over me, and now so was this woman with a lot of money. I still had respect for the kind of money she earned, having come out of it myself, and there were moments when I sensed the old man trying to resurrect.

She started calling me on the phone at night and asked if I knew the Bible? I said, "Yes, I know enough," to which she replied, "I want to ask you some questions about the Bible..."

Praise the Lord. Every question she asked, God gave me the answer. She was amazed and said, "You do know the Bible." Before long she called me just to talk and the Lord turned the whole situation around.

Soon the young men in the facility started asking me questions too. "What are you reading?"

"My Bible; but I can't share it with you because of rules at this facility."

This was a large, eight-bedroom house. I would go to the staff-only T.V. room and watch Christian television. One day one of the pedophiles asked if he could watch with me and I told him, "No, it's against the rules." But I did tell him that I was saved and a Christian.

He said, "Well, I want to be saved too!"

"Do you believe in Jesus?"

"Yes."

"Well, all you have to do is pray!"

Praise the Lord. I was on a mission from God, so whatever it took it was all worth it. Amen! God started moving on these young, disturbed men, twenty to thirty years of age, one by one. When a parent called, they wanted to talk to me first above all other attendants. It wasn't me they sought; it was Christ the hope and glory. One of the parents said, "You must be a Christian! You're an answer to prayer!"

God answers prayer. Each day the *Access Transportation* bus picked up the boys and took them to various places like appointments, court hearings, and so forth. The driver was a Christian who worked for the Sheriff's

Department until he was shot. Now he droves buses but his leg still gave him a problem. So one day we prayed together on the porch whereupon he rejoiced.

But the devil is always busy. The young lady whom I rejected when she snuck into my room reported me to the director's office and said that I was "having prayer meetings inside the house," which was against the rules. She lied.

I was approached by the psychologist who, before she said anything, told me that she really liked me, but that she also had to do her job. She said, "I was told that you're having prayer meetings in the house..."

I asked, "Who said that?" but she would not tell me.

"Okay, well, I quit, no problem."

She pleaded, "No, Bruce, please don't quit! You're the best she has here, I beg you to not quit!"

I said, "First of all, I did not do that and I would not. I have respect; I am a Christian!"

"Yes, I know that, we all know that and we respect you!"

"Then let me do what's best and leave."

After that, the owner came and offered me more money to stay. I worked an extra week until she found a replacement. Donald was the young man who received the Lord cried and said over and over, "I need you in my life, don't leave!" All the pedophiles cried. What would become of them now?

Looking back, perhaps I should have stayed, but if there is one thing that I cannot stand in this world, it's to be falsely accused. I'm not perfect.

Chapter 16

The God School

In 2001, I was on a mission from God when I went to Houston, Texas, to minister and work at one of five charter schools. I was to council students and create positive changes I their lives. The charter schools were Juvenile Halls, of sorts, with a Christian anointing. I came upon this three-month position through some of the church mothers I had met.

My first impression of the school was how frightening it was, and how all the young people there were in dire need of help. In my heart I could hear their cries for help. For them, life was a war zone. Emotionally killed in action long ago, they continued breathing, mechanically, without life-support, wondering why they were ever born. Our cities and towns are filled with children like this. Looking at the big picture I saw lost, little girls dressed like prostitutes, and boys acting like gangsters, but secretly were too afraid to get out of bed in the morning. It was extremely sad for me to watch these out of control kids, labeled at-risk, due to no fault of their own. Kids like this don't grow on trees. There was no doubt in my mind who had done this to them -- the most dangerous creatures on Earth— their parents.

I and two other female ministers did our part to help these children but at times it was so bad, the Houston police, who also worked there, were called in to keep the peace. My duties entailed patrolling the hallways to make sure the kids were in class, working with the principal when there were issues with students or parents, and attending teacher meetings.

Before long the other staff members perceived that I had the certain gift of resolving problems effectively. One day the principal asked me to work in the detention room, where kids were sent who got kicked out of class. The first time I worked detention involved about twelve kids and I knew right away, the appointment was set by God.

The first thing I did was introduce myself and share my purpose for being there. Then, I asked each kid to stand up, say their name and tell the class what they like to do for fun.

"Do any of you have any talents like singing, dancing, rap, poetry, or just tell us about yourself. Why were you put out of class?"

One little girl stood up and recited a beautiful poem that she wrote whereupon a hush fell upon the entire room. Then she said matter-of-factly, "I don't come to school that much because I need clothes and shoes. I'm wearing my house-shoes right now. Plus, my mother is on crack-cocaine and she's never at home."

For me, this was sad beyond measure, especially when I think about some of these ridiculous, reality-TV starlets prancing about Hollywood, so privileged and wealthy, and on the other spectrum, we've got kids in our own country that don't even have school shoes.

The young student then pointed to another girl and said, "She shouldn't be in here. She has a big, pretty house, a good mother and father. She's so lucky!"

I listened to the kids' heartbreaking honesty as one by one they opened up. The result was that they started helping each other by telling the truth and being honest.

Then, all of them said, "Can we do this every day?"

I laughed and said, "Well, this is detention! Do you guys plan on getting kicked out of class every day?"

They laughed and said, "Yeah, but we need this. It's helping us to talk about our problems." I told them that my job was to help them so that they can help each other.

The presiding pastor of the school had been approved for $60 Million in grant funding to open five of these charter schools, but as it goes many times with men of God who do great works, persecution soon shows up at the door. It didn't take long for newspapers to allege that the pastor was engaged in illegal activity. Allegations were also made that he had millions of the grant money stashed beneath his house.

I never witnessed anything other than the pastor and his dedicated staff help the kids stay out of trouble. These secular trouble-makers are what we call 'the accusers of the brethren.' Personally I liked the pastor. I can barely go anywhere without the Lord showing me something bad about someone, but the Lord didn't do so with this pastor. He checked out alright with the Lord and me.

Because of my work with the kids, those that hardly ever came to school were now in regular attendance, and I let them know that I was very proud of their changes.

Some of them confided in me that they were selling drugs and then stopped doing so. I believe that because I showed just a little bit of interest in their lives, it gave them hope and a new outlook on life ahead. If that's what just a little bit of interest from a perfect stranger can do, imagine how drastically their lives would alter, perhaps beyond recognition, with regular doses of caring from their own, absent parents?

Thank God that we have a true Father in Heaven, who never leaves us nor forsakes us.

Chapter 17

Strange Callings

Recall the day when all this got started...I was walking down the street naked, wrapped in a sheet, with long, dripping-wet hair and bare feet. I saw the shock on my poor mother's face as she opened the door.

"My God! My son's walkin' into my house with nothin' but a sheet on?! He' gone *crazy!*"

Years later I did tell my parents what happened that day but I could barely find the words. At the time I was not yet studied in the word to put the event it into ecclesiastic context, let alone the prophetic. My mother was a strong, country woman who never bit her tongue. She always just hauled off and said anything she pleased.

"If its God, you will change...but you know insanity runs in your family."

I just laughed. My Dad believed me, however. The only thing he said was, "You're called to preach."

My mother continued, "I heard your Uncle Neal went crazy, telling all the family members they better get saved..."

Neal was my mother's brother. With thirteen siblings in her family, Uncle Neal was my favorite. She said he got saved but I didn't know what that meant.

"Saved from what?"

Shortly thereafter, I met up with my Uncle Neal and he shared with me his own salvation experience. It turns out that five months before my own bed-sheet experience, he received the Lord in an equally unusual manner.

He used to go to the race-track to gamble all the time, but this one day at the track was different. After placing his bet and ordering a beer, he sat back and prepared for another great day of aimless libations. The race bell rang and the horses took off. Suddenly, he heard a loud smash of thunder!

There was a man standing next to him, so Uncle Neal called out to him, "Man, that thunder was loud, eh? I guess it's gonna' rain!" But the man shrugged his shoulders and irritated, he said, "I didn't hear anything," and proceeded to walk away from my uncle. Then Uncle Neal said he heard a booming, loud voice command, "PRAISE ME!"

That's when Uncle Neal put down the beer and started to tremble. Before he knew it, his hand shot up in the air, involuntarily, and he couldn't bring it back down! His arm refused to budge so he kept repeating, "Oh God, oh God!"

He thought, "If I count to three maybe my hand will come down." By now the man who walked away earlier must have been watching all this from afar. Then Uncle Neal counted to three and it thundered again. This time his arm came down.

The experience scared Uncle Neal to death and he stopped going to the race-track all together. After that Uncle Neal and I became very close because both of us received supernatural visitations from which neither of recovered, in the best sense.

Praise God, Uncle Neal went home to be with the Lord in 2010. He was eighty-two years old. After I told Uncle Neal about all that happened to me, he never stopped telling my mother that it was God who called me, until the day he died.

My father also went home to be with the Lord while at work, on May 9, 1980; one day after my mother's birthday. After his parting, I took care of my dear mother for seven years until she also went to the Lord in 1987.

My Mom and Dad in 1944

PART 4

Innocence Lost

Happy are those who reject the advice of evil people, who do not follow the example of sinners, or join those who have no use for God.

Psalms 1:1

Chapter 18

Las Vegas 1969

All my life, I have shopped at exclusive, men's clothing stores, even back in junior high school, as you'll see in the photo on the next page. Style is very important to me; it expresses who I am. In fact, I started buying and selling clothes at the age of seventeen. As a self-respecting person, I also have great respect for other people. We are all so different, and I was blessed to have the ability throughout my lifetime to pay attention to people, to observe and study them, closely and patiently. I guess you could say that I'm a people-watcher.

Through patience I learned important values. I remember playing little league baseball and the coach took

15 yrs

us kids out for ice-cream, about twelve of us. Everybody crowded around the ice-cream counter trying to be first and yelling at the ice-cream man, but I didn't move at all. As a result of good, home-training, I stayed behind in the back row and waited my turn. When the ice-cream man noticed this, he told me that he was proud of me and gave me more ice cream than everyone else. I learned a good lesson that day, but in 1969, I learned a bad lesson.

Life gives us a story all our own. Having given you a picture of mine will help you to understand me, and my sensitive, conscientious side.

In 1969, I was enrolled at Don Martin School of Broadcasting, in Hollywood, California. I had just passed the FCC test for my first-class, engineering license. During my lunch hour, I walked around the corner to an art studio. I'm an artist, but had never worked with oil paints before, so I enrolled in art lessons to learn how to work with oils. On the first day of class, I painted a picture so well, the instructor said, "You don't need any more lessons. Help us finish this project in Las Vegas."

So I took the offer and moved to Las Vegas temporarily. The project entailed painting murals on commercial buildings so I started the job by drawing up all the layout sketches. The place was called, *African Imports Art Gallery*. The person who set up the project was Bob Bailey, cousin of the famous Pearl Bailey. Bob Bailey was the first Black councilman in Las Vegas during the early 1960s. He also owned two nightclubs: the *Comedy Club*, *Sugarhill* and *Colony Club*. He was also a licensed real estate broker, and owned a youth training center called C.E.P.; the acronyms of which I can no longer recall. The C.E.P. Center prepared minority youth to work in Las Vegas doing custodial work, because they didn't hire Blacks in the casinos back in those days as dealers or other gaming jobs.

Bob Bailey also asked me to help out at center, training the kids in broadcasting. I was only nineteen years old at that time. Bob Bailey became a good friend and mentor. He said I reminded him of himself as a young man. As a licensed engineer himself, he told me that we were the only Blacks in Las Vegas with engineering licenses.

"Neither of us will ever get jobs in that field here in Vegas, because we're Black," he insisted.

To prove it, he took me to several radio stations and they all said the same thing. "You need an engineering license," (but you really didn't if you were white.) Each time I proceeded to pull out my engineering license, silence fell upon the room with a loud thunk, followed by the interviewers' complete shock. Then they turned beet-red and were obliged to take down our phone numbers, but of course, they never called. Bob had already prepared me for this. It was 1969, only four years after the *March on Selma*. Bob waited outside when he took me to all the radio stations in Las Vegas and it was the same thing at each stop.

The hotel I was staying at asked me to paint a mural on their exterior wall. So on my days off, I set up my work station outside around the pool to paint, and people stopped by to watch. One of the women who stayed at the hotel invited me to dinner one night, and cooked me a very good, soul-food meal.

I could tell she liked and admired me. A young, Black man making money in Vegas in the 1960s was a rare commodity; but she didn't know that I was only nineteen. She called my room one night and asked if I could drop her off at a hotel on the strip. When I drove her there, I noticed that she was dressed very nicely; she looked good.

After that, I knew she was a working girl, a prostitute, at the age of thirty-nine. I wasn't in the game at that point, but I knew the game. Her name was Toni. She looked good, but she had a foul mouth. I never liked women who cussed. When I told her that, it was like a miracle. She changed overnight. Everyone that knew her could not believe it. Toni was always so loud and vulgar and then she just stopped cussing, cold turkey; just like that.

When the time came for me to return to Los Angeles, Toni didn't want me to go. She offered to take care of me and move to L.A. with me, get us a big house in Holly-wood, so on and so forth, but I couldn't fit her into my life back then. I had already made plans for my future, so I left her in Las Vegas. I had to finish my education and I was still living in my parent's house. My parents and I were very close, and I respected their values to finish my education. What would they think if were the well-kept boy of a thirty-nine year old woman?

Before I returned to Los Angeles, my mentor, Bob Bailey, asked me to meet him at his broker's office at the *Moulon Rougue*. Bob and Sonny Liston, the legendary boxer, were friends at a time when Sonny was the heavyweight champion of the world, until Cassius Clay took his title. When I got to Bob's office, there was a big mess all around; papers and trash were strewn all over the room. It turns out that the police raided his office the night before and planted drugs in his desk. As he waded through the trash, he told me the story.

"The police took me down to the station last night and booked me on drug charges, but they didn't hold me. The sergeant said they only needed me on record... and they let me go."

Then Bob hung his head in sad resignation and said, "They killed Sonny last night."

"Sonny Liston? Who killed Sonny Liston?"

"The police!"

Mr. Bob Bailey was like a father and friend to me. I will never forget what he used to say.

"Black man, whatever you do in life, be strong! We can't be quitters. Live out your dream!"

My old friend Bob never did find out that I took a wrong turn in life, but I think he'd be proud of what has become of me today.

If ever you need someone to talk to, shoot me an email. Or hey...see you on the streets of L.A.

In Closing ...

I want to personally thank everyone for taking the time to read my book of testimonies. First and foremost, I thank God Almighty in Jesus' name. Without Him, there would be no stories to tell.

Secondly, I'd like to thank my dynamic mother, Maude Henderson, and father, Stanley Henderson (the greatest man I ever knew, besides Christ) for their constant love, presence and affection throughout my life. And my daughters: Natalie Lynn Hamilton, a Registered Nurse; and my youngest, artistic daughter, Sha'ree Faith Henderson; and of course my best friend, Sweet Marie D. Smith.

Family of God, be concerned about each other. Let people know you care about them, whether it's by helping someone through a tough time, giving them food and clothing, or just a kind word. Jesus said, if we help them, we've done it to Him, personally. Therefore, your caring acts mean so much to God. Let us be doers of the word of God. Thank you.

Stanley Bruce Henderson, Jr.

Evangelist / Street Preacher

Contact Information

We hope that you enjoyed
Evangelist Bruce Henderson's rare
and astounding journey.

To order additional copies of this book
or schedule a speaking engagement,
please contact the evangelist at:

newstartmin@yahoo.com